EMMANUEL JOSEPH

The Alchemy of Holistic Success, Uniting Mind, Body, and Financial Mastery

Copyright © 2025 by Emmanuel Joseph

All rights reserved. No part of this publication may be reproduced, stored or transmitted in any form or by any means, electronic, mechanical, photocopying, recording, scanning, or otherwise without written permission from the publisher. It is illegal to copy this book, post it to a website, or distribute it by any other means without permission.

First edition

*This book was professionally typeset on Reedsy.
Find out more at reedsy.com*

Contents

1	Chapter 1: The Foundations of Holistic Success	1
2	Chapter 2: Cultivating a Growth Mindset	3
3	Chapter 3: Mindfulness and Mental Clarity	5
4	Chapter 4: The Power of Positive Thinking	7
5	Chapter 5: Embracing Physical Wellness	9
6	Chapter 6: Financial Literacy and Empowerment	11
7	Chapter 7: The Art of Networking and Building Relationships	13
8	Chapter 8: Time Management and Productivity	15
9	Chapter 9: The Role of Self-Care in Holistic Success	17
10	Chapter 10: The Journey of Personal Growth and...	19
11	Chapter 11: Achieving Work-Life Balance	21
12	Chapter 12: The Importance of Goal Setting	23
13	Chapter 13: The Role of Mentorship and Guidance	25
14	Chapter 14: Embracing Change and Innovation	27
15	Chapter 15: The Journey Towards Holistic Success	29

1

Chapter 1: The Foundations of Holistic Success

The concept of holistic success revolves around the intricate balance of mind, body, and financial mastery. This journey begins with understanding that success is multi-dimensional, requiring an integrated approach. In our fast-paced society, it's easy to compartmentalize our lives, separating professional achievements from personal well-being. Yet, true success emerges from the harmony of these facets, nurturing each one to create a fulfilling, well-rounded life.

The mind is the powerhouse of all achievements, shaping our thoughts, decisions, and actions. Cultivating a healthy mindset is crucial, involving practices like mindfulness, positive affirmations, and continuous learning. A strong mental foundation fuels resilience and adaptability, allowing us to navigate life's challenges with grace. Moreover, mental clarity enhances productivity, creativity, and problem-solving abilities, paving the way for both personal and professional growth.

Physical health serves as the vessel that carries us through our journey towards success. A balanced diet, regular exercise, and adequate rest are the cornerstones of a healthy body. Physical well-being not only boosts energy levels but also fortifies mental health. The mind and body are intrinsically connected; neglecting one impacts the other. Thus, incorporating wellness routines into our daily lives is essential for sustaining long-term success.

Financial mastery, the final piece of the puzzle, provides the stability and resources needed to pursue our dreams. Financial literacy, budgeting, and smart investments are the building blocks of economic empowerment. When we manage our finances effectively, we reduce stress and create opportunities for growth and exploration. Financial independence allows us to make choices that align with our values and passions, further enriching our holistic success.

2

Chapter 2: Cultivating a Growth Mindset

A growth mindset is the belief that abilities and intelligence can be developed through dedication and hard work. This perspective fosters a love for learning and resilience essential for achieving greatness. By embracing challenges and viewing failures as opportunities for growth, we unlock our potential. Adopting a growth mindset shifts our focus from seeking approval to continuous improvement, driving us to strive for excellence in all areas of life.

Self-awareness is the cornerstone of personal development, enabling us to identify our strengths and areas for improvement. Through introspection and reflection, we gain insights into our behaviors, motivations, and thought patterns. This heightened awareness empowers us to make intentional choices that align with our goals and values. As we become more attuned to our inner selves, we cultivate a deeper understanding of our purpose and direction.

Embracing lifelong learning is key to personal and professional growth. Staying curious and open to new experiences broadens our horizons and enhances our skill set. Whether it's reading books, attending workshops, or seeking mentorship, continuous learning keeps us adaptable and competitive in an ever-evolving world. By prioritizing education and self-improvement, we invest in our future success.

Building resilience through adversity is a crucial aspect of a growth

mindset. Life's challenges are inevitable, but our response to them defines our character. Developing resilience involves cultivating emotional intelligence, practicing self-compassion, and seeking support when needed. By overcoming obstacles, we strengthen our resolve and gain confidence in our ability to navigate uncertainties. This resilience propels us forward, transforming setbacks into stepping stones.

3

Chapter 3: Mindfulness and Mental Clarity

Mindfulness is the practice of being fully present in the moment, aware of our thoughts, feelings, and surroundings. This state of heightened awareness promotes mental clarity and emotional balance. By practicing mindfulness, we can reduce stress, enhance focus, and improve overall well-being. Techniques such as meditation, deep breathing, and mindful journaling help cultivate this essential skill, allowing us to navigate life with greater ease and intention.

Mental clarity is the ability to think clearly and make sound decisions, free from distractions and confusion. Achieving mental clarity requires us to declutter our minds and prioritize tasks effectively. This involves setting clear goals, creating structured routines, and minimizing digital distractions. By simplifying our lives and focusing on what truly matters, we can enhance our cognitive abilities and make more informed choices.

Emotional regulation is an integral part of maintaining mental clarity. Recognizing and managing our emotions allows us to respond to situations calmly and rationally. Practices such as emotional journaling, seeking therapy, and engaging in creative outlets can help us process our feelings and maintain a balanced state of mind. Emotional regulation not only improves mental clarity but also strengthens our relationships and overall well-being.

Creating a conducive environment for mental clarity involves both physical and mental spaces. Organizing our surroundings, establishing designated work areas, and maintaining a clean, clutter-free space can enhance focus and productivity. Similarly, fostering a positive mental environment by surrounding ourselves with supportive individuals and engaging in uplifting activities can further promote mental clarity. By prioritizing both external and internal environments, we set the stage for optimal cognitive function.

4

Chapter 4: The Power of Positive Thinking

Positive thinking is the practice of focusing on the good in any given situation, fostering an optimistic outlook. This mindset shift can significantly impact our overall well-being and success. By cultivating gratitude, affirmations, and visualization, we can rewire our brains to see opportunities rather than obstacles. Positive thinking not only enhances our mental health but also attracts positive outcomes, creating a cycle of success and fulfillment.

Gratitude is a powerful tool for fostering positivity and resilience. By regularly acknowledging and appreciating the good in our lives, we can shift our focus away from negativity and cultivate a sense of abundance. Gratitude journaling, expressing thanks to others, and practicing mindfulness can help embed this practice into our daily lives. This shift in perspective not only improves our mood but also strengthens our relationships and overall satisfaction with life.

Affirmations are positive statements that can help reframe our mindset and boost self-confidence. By repeating affirmations, we can challenge and overcome self-sabotaging thoughts. Crafting personalized affirmations that resonate with our goals and values can create a powerful mental framework for success. Consistently practicing affirmations can reprogram our subconscious mind, aligning our thoughts with our desired outcomes.

Visualization is the process of mentally rehearsing desired outcomes, enhancing our ability to achieve them. By vividly imagining our goals and the steps required to reach them, we can create a mental blueprint for success. Visualization can increase motivation, focus, and self-efficacy, making it easier to turn our dreams into reality. Incorporating visualization into our daily routine can help us stay aligned with our goals and maintain a positive mindset.

5

Chapter 5: Embracing Physical Wellness

Physical wellness is a crucial component of holistic success, providing the foundation for mental and emotional well-being. Regular exercise, a balanced diet, and adequate sleep are essential for maintaining optimal health. By prioritizing physical wellness, we can boost our energy levels, improve our mood, and enhance our overall quality of life. Incorporating these habits into our daily routine can set the stage for long-term success.

Exercise is vital for maintaining physical health and well-being. Regular physical activity can improve cardiovascular health, strengthen muscles, and enhance flexibility. Exercise also releases endorphins, which can boost our mood and reduce stress. Finding activities that we enjoy, such as dancing, swimming, or hiking, can make exercise a fun and sustainable part of our routine.

Nutrition plays a significant role in our overall health and well-being. A balanced diet, rich in fruits, vegetables, lean proteins, and whole grains, can provide the essential nutrients our bodies need to function optimally. By making mindful food choices and avoiding processed foods, we can fuel our bodies for success. Staying hydrated and practicing portion control are also key components of a healthy diet.

Sleep is often overlooked but is a critical aspect of physical wellness. Adequate rest is essential for our bodies to recover and recharge. Quality sleep can improve cognitive function, boost immunity, and enhance emotional resilience. Establishing a consistent sleep schedule, creating a relaxing bedtime routine, and minimizing screen time before bed can help improve sleep quality. Prioritizing rest ensures that we are physically and mentally prepared to tackle our goals.

6

Chapter 6: Financial Literacy and Empowerment

Financial literacy is the knowledge and skills needed to make informed and effective decisions about money management. Understanding the basics of budgeting, saving, and investing can provide a strong foundation for financial success. By becoming financially literate, we can take control of our economic future, reduce stress, and create opportunities for growth and security.

Budgeting is the process of creating a plan for how to spend and save money. By tracking our income and expenses, we can make informed decisions about our finances and prioritize our spending. A well-crafted budget can help us manage debt, save for future goals, and avoid financial pitfalls. Regularly reviewing and adjusting our budget ensures that we stay on track and make progress towards our financial objectives.

Saving is an essential aspect of financial empowerment, providing a safety net for unexpected expenses and future goals. Establishing an emergency fund and setting aside money for short-term and long-term objectives can create a sense of financial security. Automating savings and cutting unnecessary expenses can help build a robust financial cushion. Saving consistently, even in small amounts, can lead to significant growth over time.

Investing is the process of using money to generate returns and build wealth. Understanding the basics of investing, such as stocks, bonds, and real estate, can help us make informed decisions about growing our wealth. Diversifying our investments and seeking professional advice can mitigate risks and maximize returns. By investing wisely, we can create opportunities for financial independence and long-term success.

7

Chapter 7: The Art of Networking and Building Relationships

Networking and building strong relationships are essential for personal and professional success. Cultivating a supportive network can provide valuable opportunities, resources, and connections. Effective networking involves genuine interactions, active listening, and mutual support. By nurturing relationships, we create a community of like-minded individuals who can help us achieve our goals and navigate challenges.

Effective communication is the foundation of strong relationships. Developing good communication skills, such as active listening, empathy, and clarity, can enhance our interactions with others. Building rapport and trust through open and honest communication fosters deeper connections. By being present and attentive in our conversations, we can create meaningful and lasting relationships.

Mutual support and collaboration are key components of successful networking. Offering help and support to others can strengthen our relationships and create a sense of reciprocity. By sharing knowledge, resources, and opportunities, we can build a network based on trust and mutual benefit. Collaboration fosters innovation and growth, enabling us to achieve more together than we could alone.

Maintaining relationships requires effort and consistency. Regularly reaching out, expressing appreciation, and staying connected can help sustain our network. Celebrating successes, offering encouragement during challenges, and being there for important milestones can deepen our bonds. By investing time and energy into our relationships, we create a supportive and empowering network that contributes to our holistic success.

8

Chapter 8: Time Management and Productivity

Effective time management is crucial for achieving our goals and maintaining a balanced life. By prioritizing tasks, setting goals, and creating structured routines, we can make the most of our time. Effective time management reduces stress, increases productivity, and creates a sense of accomplishment. By mastering this skill, we can achieve our goals while maintaining a healthy work-life balance.

Setting clear and achievable goals is the first step in effective time management. By defining our objectives and breaking them down into smaller tasks, we can create a roadmap for success. SMART goals—Specific, Measurable, Achievable, Relevant, and Time-bound—provide a clear framework for progress. Regularly reviewing and adjusting our goals ensures that we stay on track and make meaningful progress.

Creating structured routines and schedules can help us manage our time effectively. By allocating specific time blocks for tasks, we can minimize distractions and stay focused. Tools such as calendars, to-do lists, and productivity apps can assist in organizing our time. Establishing daily, weekly, and monthly routines creates consistency and helps us develop productive habits.

Minimizing distractions and staying focused are essential for maxi-

mizing productivity. Identifying and eliminating time-wasting activities, such as excessive screen time or multitasking, can enhance our efficiency. Creating a dedicated workspace, practicing mindfulness, and setting boundaries can help us stay focused. By prioritizing our tasks and eliminating distractions, we can accomplish more in less time.

9

Chapter 9: The Role of Self-Care in Holistic Success

Self-care is the practice of prioritizing our physical, mental, and emotional well-being. Incorporating self-care into our daily routine is essential for maintaining a balanced and fulfilling life. Self-care practices, such as exercise, relaxation, and hobbies, provide a respite from stress and enhance our overall well-being. By prioritizing self-care, we can recharge and maintain the energy needed for holistic success.

Physical self-care involves activities that improve our physical health and well-being. Regular exercise, a balanced diet, and adequate sleep are fundamental aspects of physical self-care. Incorporating activities such as yoga, meditation, and outdoor adventures can enhance our physical health. By prioritizing physical self-care, we can boost our energy levels and improve our overall quality of life.

Mental self-care focuses on activities that stimulate and rejuvenate our minds. Practices such as reading, journaling, and engaging in creative pursuits can enhance our mental well-being. Taking breaks, practicing mindfulness, and seeking professional support when needed are also important aspects of mental self-care. By nurturing our minds, we can improve our cognitive abilities and emotional resilience.

Emotional self-care involves activities that nurture our emotional

health and well-being. Building healthy relationships, practicing gratitude, and engaging in activities that bring joy and fulfillment are essential for emotional self-care. Seeking therapy, practicing self-compassion, and setting boundaries can help us manage our emotions effectively. By prioritizing emotional self-care, we can cultivate a sense of inner peace and happiness.

10

Chapter 10: The Journey of Personal Growth and Transformation

Personal growth and transformation are ongoing processes that involve self-discovery, learning, and change. Embracing these processes can lead to a more fulfilling and successful life. Personal growth involves setting goals, overcoming challenges, and continuously improving ourselves. By committing to personal growth, we can unlock our potential and achieve holistic success.

Self-discovery is the process of understanding our values, strengths, and passions. Through introspection, reflection, and exploration, we can gain insights into our true selves. This self-awareness enables us to make choices that align with our values and purpose. By embracing self-discovery, we can create a life that reflects our authentic selves.

Learning is a lifelong journey that enhances our knowledge, skills, and abilities. Staying curious and open to new experiences can broaden our horizons and keep us adaptable in a changing world. Whether through formal education, self-study, or experiential learning, continuous learning fosters personal and professional growth. By prioritizing education, we invest in our future success.

Transformation involves overcoming challenges and embracing change. Life's obstacles can be opportunities for growth and development.

By developing resilience, practicing self-compassion, and seeking support, we can navigate challenges effectively. Embracing change and stepping out of our comfort zones can lead to transformative experiences. By committing to personal growth and transformation, we can achieve our full potential.

11

Chapter 11: Achieving Work-Life Balance

Work-life balance is the equilibrium between professional responsibilities and personal activities. Striking this balance is crucial for overall well-being and long-term success. By setting boundaries, prioritizing self-care, and managing time effectively, we can achieve a harmonious work-life balance. This balance not only enhances productivity but also improves our quality of life and relationships.

Setting boundaries is essential for maintaining work-life balance. Clearly defining work hours, personal time, and family commitments can help create a sense of structure. Communicating these boundaries to colleagues and loved ones ensures that they are respected. By setting limits and prioritizing our time, we can prevent burnout and maintain a healthy balance between work and personal life.

Prioritizing self-care is key to achieving work-life balance. Incorporating activities that promote physical, mental, and emotional well-being into our daily routine can recharge our energy levels. Taking breaks, practicing mindfulness, and engaging in hobbies can help us unwind and relax. By prioritizing self-care, we can maintain the stamina needed to fulfill our professional and personal responsibilities.

Effective time management is crucial for balancing work and personal life. Creating a structured schedule that allocates time for work, family, and leisure activities can help us stay organized. Utilizing tools such as calendars, planners, and productivity apps can enhance our time management skills. By managing our time effectively, we can achieve our goals while maintaining a fulfilling personal life.

12

Chapter 12: The Importance of Goal Setting

Goal setting is the process of defining and planning for desired outcomes. Setting clear and achievable goals provides direction, motivation, and a sense of purpose. By creating a roadmap for success, we can track our progress and stay focused on our objectives. Goal setting is a powerful tool for personal and professional growth, enabling us to achieve our dreams.

SMART goals are Specific, Measurable, Achievable, Relevant, and Time-bound. This framework provides a clear structure for setting and achieving goals. Specific goals define clear outcomes, while measurable goals allow us to track progress. Achievable goals are realistic and attainable, and relevant goals align with our values and long-term aspirations. Time-bound goals have a defined timeline, creating a sense of urgency and accountability.

Regularly reviewing and adjusting our goals ensures that we stay on track and make meaningful progress. Reflecting on our achievements, challenges, and areas for improvement can provide valuable insights. Adjusting our goals based on these reflections ensures that they remain relevant and attainable. By continuously evaluating our goals, we can stay motivated and committed to our personal and professional growth.

**Celebrating successes and milestones is an important aspect of goal

setting. Acknowledging and rewarding our achievements, no matter how small, can boost our motivation and self-confidence. Celebrating successes also provides an opportunity to reflect on our journey and appreciate the progress we have made. By recognizing our accomplishments, we reinforce positive behaviors and maintain momentum towards our goals.

13

Chapter 13: The Role of Mentorship and Guidance

Mentorship and guidance are invaluable resources for personal and professional development. A mentor provides support, advice, and insights based on their experiences and expertise. Building a relationship with a mentor can enhance our knowledge, skills, and confidence. By seeking mentorship, we can gain valuable perspectives and guidance on our journey towards holistic success.

Finding the right mentor involves identifying individuals who align with our goals and values. A mentor should possess the expertise, experience, and qualities that resonate with our aspirations. Seeking mentorship from diverse sources, such as colleagues, industry leaders, or community members, can provide a well-rounded perspective. Building a strong mentor-mentee relationship involves open communication, mutual respect, and trust.

Mentorship offers numerous benefits, including knowledge sharing, skill development, and networking opportunities. A mentor can provide valuable insights, constructive feedback, and practical advice based on their experiences. This guidance can help us navigate challenges, make informed decisions, and avoid common pitfalls. Additionally, a mentor's network can open doors to new opportunities and connections.

Giving back through mentorship is a rewarding way to contribute to the growth and success of others. By sharing our knowledge and experiences, we can support and inspire the next generation of leaders. Mentoring others also reinforces our own learning and growth, creating a positive cycle of development. By fostering a culture of mentorship, we can create a supportive and empowering community that values personal and professional growth.

14

Chapter 14: Embracing Change and Innovation

Change and innovation are essential for growth and success in an ever-evolving world. Embracing change involves adapting to new circumstances, learning from experiences, and seeking opportunities for improvement. Innovation requires creativity, open-mindedness, and a willingness to take risks. By embracing change and fostering innovation, we can stay relevant, competitive, and successful.

Adapting to change involves developing resilience, flexibility, and a proactive mindset. Viewing change as an opportunity for growth rather than a threat can shift our perspective. Embracing change requires us to let go of old habits and embrace new possibilities. By staying open to change, we can navigate uncertainties and seize opportunities for personal and professional growth.

Fostering innovation involves cultivating a creative and open-minded approach to problem-solving. Encouraging curiosity, experimentation, and out-of-the-box thinking can lead to innovative solutions. Creating an environment that supports and rewards innovation can inspire individuals to think creatively and challenge the status quo. By embracing innovation, we can drive progress and stay ahead of the curve.

**Taking calculated risks is an integral part of embracing change and

innovation. Assessing potential risks and rewards, and making informed decisions, can lead to new opportunities and breakthroughs. By stepping out of our comfort zones and taking strategic risks, we can achieve significant growth and success. Learning from failures and setbacks is also crucial, as they provide valuable insights and pave the way for future success.

15

Chapter 15: The Journey Towards Holistic Success

The journey towards holistic success is a continuous process of growth, learning, and self-discovery. By uniting mind, body, and financial mastery, we can achieve a balanced and fulfilling life. Holistic success requires commitment, perseverance, and a willingness to embrace change. By nurturing all aspects of our lives, we create a foundation for long-term happiness and success.

Reflecting on our journey allows us to appreciate the progress we have made and the lessons we have learned. Regular introspection and evaluation can provide valuable insights into our strengths, areas for improvement, and future aspirations. By acknowledging our achievements and learning from our experiences, we can stay motivated and focused on our goals.

Maintaining a balanced approach to success involves continuously nurturing our mind, body, and financial well-being. Prioritizing self-care, lifelong learning, and financial empowerment ensures that we stay on track. By integrating these practices into our daily lives, we can create a sustainable foundation for holistic success.

Inspiring and supporting others on their journey towards holistic success can create a positive ripple effect. Sharing our experiences, knowledge, and resources can empower others to achieve their goals. By fostering a culture of collaboration and mutual support, we can create a community that values holistic success. Together, we can achieve greatness and contribute to a brighter future.

Book Description: The Alchemy of Holistic Success: Uniting Mind, Body, and Financial Mastery is a compelling guide that explores the intricate balance required to achieve true success. This book delves into the interconnectedness of mental, physical, and financial well-being, emphasizing the importance of nurturing each aspect to create a fulfilling and well-rounded life.

Through fifteen insightful chapters, the book covers a wide range of topics, including cultivating a growth mindset, practicing mindfulness, embracing physical wellness, and achieving financial empowerment. It offers practical advice, strategies, and techniques to help readers develop a holistic approach to success.

The journey begins by laying the foundations of holistic success, highlighting the significance of integrating mind, body, and financial mastery. It then explores the power of positive thinking, the art of networking, time management, and the role of self-care in maintaining balance. The book also emphasizes the importance of mentorship, goal setting, and embracing change and innovation.

Each chapter is designed to provide readers with actionable steps and insights to enhance their personal and professional lives. By uniting these essential elements, the book aims to guide readers on a transformative journey towards holistic success, empowering them to achieve their full potential and create a life of happiness, fulfillment, and prosperity.

www.ingramcontent.com/pod-product-compliance
Lightning Source LLC
LaVergne TN
LVHW020502080526
838202LV00057B/6114